THIS BOOK BELONGS TO:

_____

DATE: _____   DAY OF THE WEEK   S M T W T F S

I am ungrateful for:

These people can suck it:

These people rock:

I am actually fucking grateful for:

My list of Nope:

My list of Hope:

Fuck the following shit:

DATE: _____   DAY OF THE WEEK   S M T W T F S

Things I wish I could have said today:

Yay! I didn't fuck these things up:

On the shit list today:

Asshat of the day:

Do it Today:

Fuck it:

Today I am happy to report:

DATE: _____   DAY OF THE WEEK   S M T W T F S

Can you belive this fuckery:

Shit I gotta let go:

Shit I gotta hold on to:

Shit that is in my control:

day in a word: _____

Shit I need to do:

Shit I will never do:

Picture this:

DATE: _____ DAY OF THE WEEK   S M T W T F S

Get the venom out:

_____
_____
_____
_____
_____
_____
_____
_____
_____
_____
_____
_____
_____
_____
_____
_____
_____
_____

Hippo-twatamus of the Day:

Clusterfuck of the day:

Self care list:

Don't care list:

At least this shit doesn't suck:

DATE: _____   DAY OF THE WEEK   S M T W T F S

So glad I didn't:

What I should have said was:

Yes. I fucking can:

What the fuck was I thinking?

Assholes:

Angels:

DATE: _____   DAY OF THE WEEK   S M T W T F S

Today's Rant:

I'm loving this shit:

I am so over this crap:

shit to remember:

Some random shit:

This crap matters:

Why the fuck do people do this:

DATE: _____   DAY OF THE WEEK   S M T W T F S

Ugh:

Things I find fucking funny as hell:

Today I can't even:

Say something naughty:

Say something nice:

I am so god-damned cranky about:

DATE: _____   DAY OF THE WEEK   S M T W T F S

I am ungrateful for:

These people can suck it: ## These people rock:

I am actually fucking grateful for:

My list of Nope:

My list of Hope:

Fuck the following shit:

DATE: _____   DAY OF THE WEEK   S M T W T F S

Things I wish I could have said today:

Yay! I didn't fuck these things up:

On the shit list today: ## Asshat of the day:

Do it Today:

Fuck it:

Today I am happy to report:

DATE: _____   DAY OF THE WEEK   S M T W T F S

Can you belive this fuckery:

Shit I gotta let go:

Shit I gotta hold on to:

Shit that is in my control:

Today in a word: _____

Shit I need to do:

Shit I will never do:

Picture this:

DATE: _____   DAY OF THE WEEK   S M T W T F S

Get the venom out:

Hippo-twatamus of the Day:

Clusterfuck of the day:

Self care list:

Don't care list:

At least this shit doesn't suck:

DATE: _____   DAY OF THE WEEK   S M T W T F S

So glad I didn't:

What I should have said was:

Yes. I fucking can:

What the fuck was I thinking?

Assholes:

Angels:

DATE: _____   DAY OF THE WEEK   S M T W T F S

Today's Rant:

I'm loving this shit:

I am so over this crap:

shit to remember:

Some random shit:

This crap matters:

Why the fuck do people do this:

DATE: _____   DAY OF THE WEEK   S M T W T F S

Ugh:

Things I find fucking funny as hell:

Today I can't even:

Say something naughty:

Say something nice:

I am so god-damned cranky about:

DATE: _____   DAY OF THE WEEK   S M T W T F S

I am ungrateful for:

These people can suck it:

These people rock:

I am actually fucking grateful for:

My list of Nope:

My list of Hope:

Fuck the following shit:

DATE: _____   DAY OF THE WEEK   S M T W T F S

Things I wish I could have said today:

Yay! I didn't fuck these things up:

On the shit list today:

Asshat of the day:

Do it Today:

Fuck it:

Today I am happy to report:

DATE: _____ DAY OF THE WEEK   S M T W T F S

Can you belive this fuckery:

Shit I gotta let go:

Shit I gotta hold on to:

Shit that is in my control:

day in a word: _____

Shit I need to do:

Shit I will never do:

Picture this:

DATE: _____   DAY OF THE WEEK   S M T W T F S

Get the venom out:

Hippo-twatamus of the Day:

Clusterfuck of the day:

Self care list:

Don't care list:

At least this shit doesn't suck:

DATE: _____ DAY OF THE WEEK   S M T W T F S

So glad I didn't:

What I should have said was:

Yes. I fucking can:

What the fuck was I thinking?

Assholes:

Angels:

DATE: _____ DAY OF THE WEEK   S M T W T F S

Today's Rant:

I'm loving this shit:

I am so over this crap:

shit to remember:

Some random shit:

This crap matters:

Why the fuck do people do this:

DATE: _____   DAY OF THE WEEK   S M T W T F S

Ugh:

Things I find fucking funny as hell:

Today I can't even:

Say something naughty:

Say something nice:

I am so god-damned cranky about:

DATE: _____   DAY OF THE WEEK   S M T W T F S

I am ungrateful for:

These people can suck it:

These people rock:

I am actually fucking grateful for:

My list of Nope:

My list of Hope:

Fuck the following shit:

DATE: _____   DAY OF THE WEEK   S M T W T F S

Things I wish I could have said today:

Yay! I didn't fuck these things up:

On the shit list today:

Asshat of the day:

Do it Today:

Fuck it:

Today I am happy to report:

DATE: _____   DAY OF THE WEEK   S M T W T F S

Can you belive this fuckery:

Shit I gotta let go:

Shit I gotta hold on to:

Shit that is in my control:

day in a word: _____

Shit I need to do:

Shit I will never do:

Picture this:

DATE: _____   DAY OF THE WEEK   S M T W T F S

Get the venom out:

Hippo-twatamus of the Day:

Clusterfuck of the day:

Self care list:

Don't care list:

At least this shit doesn't suck:

DATE: _____   DAY OF THE WEEK   S M T W T F S

So glad I didn't:

What I should have said was:

Yes. I fucking can:

What the fuck was I thinking?

Assholes:

Angels:

DATE: _____ DAY OF THE WEEK   S M T W T F S

Today's Rant:

I'm loving this shit:

I am so over this crap:

shit to remember:

Some random shit:

This crap matters:

Why the fuck do people do this:

DATE: _____   DAY OF THE WEEK   S M T W T F S

Ugh:

Things I find fucking funny as hell:

Today I can't even:

Say something naughty:

Say something nice:

I am so god-damned cranky about:

DATE: _____ DAY OF THE WEEK   S M T W T F S

I am ungrateful for:

These people can suck it:

These people rock:

I am actually fucking grateful for:

My list of Nope:

My list of Hope:

Fuck the following shit:

DATE: _____   DAY OF THE WEEK   S M T W T F S

Things I wish I could have said today:

Yay! I didn't fuck these things up:

On the shit list today:

Asshat of the day:

Do it Today:

Fuck it:

Today I am happy to report:

DATE: _____   DAY OF THE WEEK   S M T W T F S

Can you belive this fuckery:

Shit I gotta let go:

Shit I gotta hold on to:

Shit that is in my control:

oday in a word: _____

Shit I need to do:

Shit I will never do:

Picture this:

DATE: _____   DAY OF THE WEEK   S M T W T F S

Get the venom out:

Hippo-twatamus of the Day:

Clusterfuck of the day:

Self care list:

Don't care list:

At least this shit doesn't suck:

DATE: _____   DAY OF THE WEEK   S M T W T F S

So glad I didn't:

What I should have said was:

Yes. I fucking can:

What the fuck was I thinking?

Assholes:

Angels:

DATE: _____   DAY OF THE WEEK   S M T W T F S

Today's Rant:

I'm loving this shit:

I am so over this crap:

shit to remember:

Some random shit:

This crap matters:

Why the fuck do people do this:

DATE: _____   DAY OF THE WEEK   S M T W T F S

Ugh:

Things I find fucking funny as hell:

Today I can't even:

Say something naughty:

Say something nice:

I am so god-damned cranky about:

DATE: _____ DAY OF THE WEEK   S M T W T F S

I am ungrateful for:

These people can suck it:

These people rock:

I am actually fucking grateful for:

My list of Nope:

My list of Hope:

Fuck the following shit:

DATE: _____   DAY OF THE WEEK   S M T W T F S

Things I wish I could have said today:

Yay! I didn't fuck these things up:

On the shit list today:

Asshat of the day:

Do it Today:

Fuck it:

Today I am happy to report:

DATE: _____   DAY OF THE WEEK   S M T W T F S

Can you belive this fuckery:

_____
_____
_____
_____
_____
_____
_____

Shit I gotta let go:

_____
_____
_____
_____
_____

Shit I gotta hold on to:

_____
_____
_____
_____
_____

Shit that is in my control:

_____
_____
_____
_____
_____

Today in a word: _____

Shit I need to do:

Shit I will never do:

Picture this:

DATE: _____   DAY OF THE WEEK   S M T W T F S

Get the venom out:

Hippo-twatamus of the Day:

Clusterfuck of the day:

Self care list:

Don't care list:

At least this shit doesn't suck:

DATE: _____   DAY OF THE WEEK   S M T W T F S

So glad I didn't:

What I should have said was:

Yes. I fucking can:

What the fuck was I thinking?

Assholes:

Angels:

DATE: _____ DAY OF THE WEEK   S M T W T F S

Today's Rant:

_____
_____
_____
_____
_____
_____

I'm loving this shit:

_____
_____
_____
_____

I am so over this crap:

_____
_____
_____
_____

shit to remember:

_____
_____
_____
_____
_____

Some random shit:

This crap matters:

Why the fuck do people do this:

DATE: _____ DAY OF THE WEEK   S M T W T F S

Ugh:

Things I find fucking funny as hell:

Today I can't even:

Say something naughty:

Say something nice:

I am so god-damned cranky about:

DATE: _____   DAY OF THE WEEK   S M T W T F S

I am ungrateful for:

These people can suck it:

These people rock:

I am actually fucking grateful for:

My list of Nope:

My list of Hope:

Fuck the following shit:

DATE: _____   DAY OF THE WEEK   S M T W T F S

Things I wish I could have said today:

Yay! I didn't fuck these things up:

On the shit list today:

Asshat of the day:

Do it Today:

Fuck it:

Today I am happy to report:

DATE: _____ DAY OF THE WEEK   S M T W T F S

Can you belive this fuckery:

Shit I gotta let go:

Shit I gotta hold on to:

Shit that is in my control:

oday in a word: _____

Shit I need to do:

Shit I will never do:

Picture this:

DATE: _____   DAY OF THE WEEK   S M T W T F S

Get the venom out:

Hippo-twatamus of the Day:

Clusterfuck of the day:

Self care list:

Don't care list:

At least this shit doesn't suck:

DATE: _____   DAY OF THE WEEK   S M T W T F S

So glad I didn't:

What I should have said was:

Yes. I fucking can:

What the fuck was I thinking?

Assholes:

Angels:

DATE: _____ DAY OF THE WEEK   S M T W T F S

Today's Rant:

I'm loving this shit:

I am so over this crap:

shit to remember:

Some random shit:

This crap matters:

Why the fuck do people do this:

DATE: _____ DAY OF THE WEEK   S M T W T F S

Ugh:

Things I find fucking funny as hell:

Today I can't even:

Say something naughty:

Say something nice:

I am so god-damned cranky about:

DATE: _____   DAY OF THE WEEK   S M T W T F S

I am ungrateful for:

These people can suck it:

These people rock:

I am actually fucking grateful for:

My list of Nope:

My list of Hope:

Fuck the following shit:

DATE: _____ DAY OF THE WEEK S M T W T F S

Things I wish I could have said today:

Yay! I didn't fuck these things up:

On the shit list today:

Asshat of the day:

Do it Today:

Fuck it:

Today I am happy to report:

DATE: _____   DAY OF THE WEEK   S M T W T F S

Can you belive this fuckery:

Shit I gotta let go:

Shit I gotta hold on to:

Shit that is in my control:

Today in a word: _____

Shit I need to do:

Shit I will never do:

Picture this:

DATE: _____   DAY OF THE WEEK   S M T W T F S

Get the venom out:

Hippo-twatamus of the Day:

Clusterfuck of the day:

Self care list:

Don't care list:

At least this shit doesn't suck:

DATE: _____   DAY OF THE WEEK   S M T W T F S

So glad I didn't:

What I should have said was:

Yes. I fucking can:

What the fuck was I thinking?

Assholes:

Angels:

DATE: _____   DAY OF THE WEEK   S M T W T F S

Today's Rant:

I'm loving this shit:

I am so over this crap:

shit to remember:

Some random shit:

This crap matters:

Why the fuck do people do this:

DATE: _____ DAY OF THE WEEK   S M T W T F S

Ugh:

Things I find fucking funny as hell:

Today I can't even:

Say something naughty:

Say something nice:

I am so god-damned cranky about:

DATE: _____ DAY OF THE WEEK S M T W T F S

I am ungrateful for:

These people can suck it:

These people rock:

I am actually fucking grateful for:

My list of Nope:

My list of Hope:

Fuck the following shit:

DATE: _____   DAY OF THE WEEK   S M T W T F S

Things I wish I could have said today:

Yay! I didn't fuck these things up:

On the shit list today:

Asshat of the day:

Do it Today:

Fuck it:

Today I am happy to report:

DATE: _____   DAY OF THE WEEK   S M T W T F S

Can you belive this fuckery:

Shit I gotta let go:

Shit I gotta hold on to:

Shit that is in my control:

Today in a word: _____

Shit I need to do:

Shit I will never do:

Picture this:

Made in the USA
Las Vegas, NV
17 January 2025

16526488R00069